CÔTE D'AZUR

BONECHI

D0573400

Diffusion en Côte d'Azur:
Sté. P.E.C.
Societé Provençale d'Edition et de Cadeaux
Ilot D - z.a. de la Haute Bédoule
13240 Septèmes-les-Vallons
tél 04 91653276 - fax 04 91653279

Project and editorial conception: Casa Editrice Bonechi
Publication Manager: Monica Bonechi
Picture research and graphic design: Marco Bonechi
Editing: Simonetta Giorgi
Video layout and cover: Alberto Douglas Scotti
Translation: Paula Boomsliter
Map: Daniela Mariani

© Copyright by CASA EDITRICE BONECHI, Via Cairoli, 18/b Firenze - Italia
Tel +39 055 576841 - Fax +39 055 5000766
E-mail: bonechi@bonechi.it   Internet: www.bonechi.it

Printed in Italy by
Centro Stampa Editoriale Bonechi.

Photographs from the Archives of Casa Editrice Bonechi taken by
Gianni Dagli Orti, Paolo Giambone, Luigi Di Giovine *and* Marco Bonechi.

Page 5: Corbis-Bettmann/Upi United Press Photo by Rene Henry.

ISBN 88-8029-794-5

*   *   *

INTRODUCTION

Setting precise bounds for the Côte d'Azur is not an easy task. In truth, the Côte d'Azur is more an idea, a dream, a mirage, than a geographical location with a well-defined beginning and end. Paradoxically, it is probably easier to define the Côte d'Azur if we start with when, instead of where. The stretch of coastline running approximately from Mentone to Saint-Tropez, the natural extension of the Ligurian Riviera, has been the object of invasions and more or less pacific colonization attempts since prehistorical times. The Ligurian Bronze Age civilizations were overlaid by the artifacts of the commercial activities of the Greeks and of the Romans' strategic concerns; the proliferation of the monasteries, the incursions by the Goths, the Vandals and the Longobards, the Saracen forays, and the struggles between Guelphs and Ghibellines changed its face; the tides of history and war shifted the political allegiances of entire territories, bringing them now under the rule of the French sovereigns, now under Italian dominion.

But it was only in the 19th century that the Côte began to assume an "azur" tint, when it became the "vacation home" of the English, dethroning Italy as the ideal resort for wealthy tourists. The advice of the Scottish physician Tobias Smollet who touted the influence of the climate in the treatment of almost any malady and prescribed sea-water baths as the sterling cure for wasting sickness, sparked a series of journeys of the duration of a couple of weeks by carriage, a few days by ship or, later, some hours on a train; an exodus that in a very short time made the English language more common on the Riviera than its native French or Italian. The Côte d'Azur is a British creation: the small fishing village destined to become that Cannes we associate with high society, luxury and entertainment owes its world-wide fame to Lord Brougham, who in 1834 chose the town for the convalescence of his stricken daughter. Fifty or so years later, that which was barely a dot on the map was competing with the highly-acclaimed Monte-Carlo in celebrity and for the presence of celebrities! Beginning in 1882, Queen Victoria spent all her winters on the Riviera with her son Leopold, first in Hyères, then in Nice. Mentone was the most anglicized center along the coast, with an outstanding sanatorium, many private clinics and at least half a hundred well-known English physicians-in-residence; it even earned the title of cleanest and most efficiently-run French city conferred by the Association for the Development of Science in 1892. The metamorphosis from winter health spa, with the proper Victorian surround of devotion and charitable works, to a scintillating world of gaming and gambling, of light-heartedness and carefree living, was rapid. Abetted by a regularly-scheduled railway service assured by the comfortable cars of the Compagnie Internationale des Wagons-Lits, an abundance of green-baize tables and an all-pervading atmosphere of relaxation, the Côte d'Azur soon won itself a reputation (and, inevitably, the ill-fame as well) as an anything-goes pleasure-spot. Around the crowned heads of half of Europe and the many others who gathered on the promenades there began to gravitate gamblers and bewitching ladies in spangles and sequins, such mysterious and secretly-admired personalities as Mata Hari and La Bella Otero, Anaïs Nin; while at the Monte-Carlo Opera House the notes of Berlioz, Massenet, Ravel, Debussy and Stravinsky were emphasized by Diaghilev's choreographic fantasies danced with outstanding bravura by Pavlova and Nijinskij against the scenery and costumes of such famous artists as Picasso, Matisse, Utrillo, Braque and Derain.

Monte-Carlo in a water-color by Gustave Janet (1872).

In the interval between the two World Wars, the incoming waves from across the Channel receded before those from across the ocean. The Twenties and the Thirties first saw the arrival of F. Scott Fitzgerald and Ernest Hemingway, and then the Hollywood stars: Clark Gable, Humphrey Bogart, Rita Hayworth, John Wayne - nor must we forget Grace Kelly. And in 1946, Cannes and its palms were the setting for the baptism of the European "Hollywood". The Palais du Festival, with its colorful court of stars and starlets, celebrities and prima donnas, became the stage on which soubrettes and bikinis, show business and scandals all contributed to focussing the attention of the entire world on La Croisette. In that same year, Picasso decided to move to Antibes and Vallauris, never to really leave the Riviera again. As Renoir and Monet, Matisse and Chagall, Signac and Gross before him, the master of Malaga drew fresh inspiration from the colors of nature, from the intensity of the native faces and from the clear blue of the skies along the coast that imbued his works with the emotions of a setting that is unique in the world.

Picasso's Coast

We might say that Picasso's relationship with the Côte d'Azur was a love affair. A tormented, intense, obsessive and fruitful love story that began in the summer of 1920, when the thirty-nine-year-old artist succumbed to the enchantment of Juan-les-Pins, continued in later years through his sojourns in Cap d'Antibes and Cannes and reached its climax in 1946, when he moved first to Menerbes and then to Vallauris; it is true that Picasso betrayed her in 1958, when he "ran off" to the great Château Vauvernagues near Aix-en-Provence, but he won her over again three years later, when he moved, definitively this time, to his Mas Notre-Dame-de-Vie in the Mougins hills. The offspring of this relationship was an almost incalculable production that ranges from painting to sculpture to ceramics to drawings; from graphics to the new technical and materic experiments with Cubism.

Thousands of works, sketches, preliminary drawings are on display in the places dearest to Picasso: we may say that there does not exist

Two works displayed at the Picasso Museum in Antibes.

a corner of this coast that does not conserve some memoir of the artist's presence, from the paintings of scenes from the lives of the fishermen, to the glazed ceramics of Vallauris, to his studio in the Palais Grimaldi in Antibes.

Picasso's early Riviera production includes a series of monumental neo-classical nudes indissolubly linked to the sky and the beaches of Juan-les-Pins. It was the early Twenties; Picasso was one of the most highly-acclaimed artists in Europe. His activity had already led him far from his native Spain and had for some time gravitated around Paris. This was the period of the hot Mediterranean summers, of the Harlequins of Cap d'Antibes, of the great still-lifes of Juan-les-Pins, of the etchings conceived in Cannes. Then the Caudillo,

the civil war in his homeland, Guernica, World War II, the artist's forced "exile" in Paris during the war years. Picasso's return to the Côte d'Azur represented for him an authentic liberation, a resuscitation, a true return to life. With Françoise Gilot, whom he had met two years previously, he spent the summer of 1945 at Villa Pour Toi overlooking the tiny port of Golfe Juan; the following year a still-life and a handshake were to seal the acquisition of Picasso's first property in the small town of Menerbes.

The summer of 1946 marked a decisive turn: Picasso officially accepted the keys to the Palais Grimaldi, and moved his studio to Antibes, while he elected residence in his small La Galloise home in Vallauris. His ceramics design work, his collaboration with the Madoura ceramics works, his research into new glazing techniques resulted in the first year alone in the production of over 2000 pieces, including plates, vases and other objects, and represented the answer to many of the economic problems faced by an industrious town that had perhaps unjustly been left by the wayside. Vallauris' appreciation of its benefactor took concrete form in 1950, when Picasso was awarded honorary citizenship - which he repaid by donating to the town the statue of L'Homme à l'Agneau which today stands in the Place Paul Isnard. In 1954, Picasso's relationship with Françoise Gilot came to an end; in the same year he met Sylviette David (to whom he dedicated thirty or so drawings and paintings which lent artistic sanction to the pony-tail hair-style launched by the mythical B.B. the year before) and Jacqueline Roque. With Jacqueline, he moved to La Californie, a huge fin-de-siècle villa near Cannes, which he immediately filled with his Paysages d'intérieur, painted - so Picasso said - to cover the empty walls of the villa's enormous rooms. In 1958 came marriage, and with it purchase of the Château Vauvernagues in Aix-en-Provence. But he returned almost immediately to his beloved Côte d'Azur, to the Mougins hills mantled in cypresses and olives; and it was in this same Mas Notre-Dame-de-Vie home that one of the greatest figures in 20th century art died at age 92 on April 8, 1973.

B.B. and Saint-Tropez

Who's that smiling girl on the deck, the one with the blond pony-tail? Oh yes, she plays that bit part in Act of Love, Anatole Litvak's entry at the Festival... the wife of that young director, Roger Vadim Plemiannikov... but how many movies has she made? Five? Hmm, now that she's taken her raincoat off...

This must have been more or less the way they were thinking, those photographers who boarded the US aircraft carrier Midway, anchored off Cannes, as their flash-guns and rapid-fire shutters bombarded the Hollywood stars gathered there. And suddenly the lenses all turned away from Lana Turner and Olivia de Havilland, arm-in-arm with Edward G. Robinson and Kirk Douglas, and from all the other publicity-seeking celebrities, to focus on that slim figure and that slightly pouting look that only a few hours later would be on the front pages of half the world's magazines. Vadim's strategy had been perfect: through an irresistible crescendo of increasingly important, and increasingly audacious, roles, the Byelorussian director succeeded in only a very few years in creating what proved to be one of cinema's longest-lasting myths, what he himself defined as "the elusive dream of every respectable married man". The ideal woman, symbol at once of sensuality and malice, youth and innocence.

Brigitte Bardot (Camille Javal) was born in Paris in 1934 of a well-to-do family. At 14, she appeared on the covers of Jardin des Modes and Elle as B.B. (for it was with these initials that her father, a stern industrialist, had insisted the photos of the emerging model be published) and was noticed by movie director Marc Allegret - already well-known for his Entrée des Artistes (1938) and Blanche Fury (1947) - who at the time was working on a script with the twenty-year-old Roger Vadim. Her screen-test for Allegret didn't pan out, but it did convince Roger. They were married four years later. It was 1952: Brigitte was in the flower of her 18 years,

and Vadim began using her in minor productions in roles that were little more than walk-ons. The 1953 Cannes showcase marked the turning-point: only a few months later, Doctor at Sea, with Dirk Bogarde, won her a place in the firmament of international stardom. But the real boom came only in 1956, with Et Dieu Créa la Femme, the effect of which was not unlike that of an atomic bomb. It was B.B.'s nineteenth stint in front of the cameras; the scenery of a then almost-unknown Saint-Tropez was the backdrop for one of the greatest successes in the history of French cinema. Its frankness created a world-wide sensation that carried the Bardot-Vadim team to exhilarating box-office heights: something in the neighborhood of eight million dollars.

And for the Côte d'Azur it was like being reborn: a romantic stroll along the wave-swept beaches, or the mirage of glimpsing B.B. bathing nude in the sea off her villa of La Madrague, near Saint-Tropez, were like authentic siren-songs that attracted tourists from all over the world. The pony-tail, the close-fitting bodices and the flat shoes became the official uniform of young women in France and everywhere else. The summer vacation on the Riviera became an appointment not to be missed, with its milieu of high society, show business, luxury, entertainment and carefree living. The yachts of celebrities and jet-set personalities crowded the fishing boats off the docks, luxury hotels supplanted the traditional village homes and radically revolutionized the appearance of the area.

The Saint-Tropez promontory, which due to its natural conformation lies off the routes of the railways and the high-speed roads built near the end of the last century, those very routes that made the fortune of such localities as Cannes and Juan-les-Pins, thus surged to the front page of society news, claiming a slot high up on the hit-parade list of those à la page localities preferred by the people who count most.

Brigitte Bardot on the beach of Cannes in 1953.

Menton, panorama from the sea.

MENTON

The name Menton comes from Mont d'Othon (in turn named for the Count of Ventimiglia) and first mention of the town dates to the year 1261. Throughout the centuries, it alternated under the Italian and French flags, until Charles III of Monaco sold it, with nearby Roquebrune, to Napoleon III for the sum of four million gold francs in 1861. "I wish I lived in this land which so recalls paradise," proclaimed Lord Byron. Menton, in fact, has perhaps the mildest climate of any of the coastal towns. One of its main resources is agriculture, mainly olives and citrus fruit. Even the delicate lemon produces fruit year-round, and every year a lemon festival is held. The other resource of the town is tourism. The **Palais de l'Europe**, a former casino built in 1909 and now refurbished, is used for congresses and hosts cultural and artistic events such as the International Biennial of Art. The winning Biennial entries are displayed in the Palais Carnolès, an art museum also containing a fine collection of paintings dating from the 14th century to our days. In 1949 the first International Chamber Music Festival was held in Menton. The world's greatest soloists and chamber music ensembles are featured each year. This city, which has preserved its slightly old-fashioned ambience, is nevertheless being developed to the utmost. A man-made beach of fine-grain sand has been put in; the promenade, the liveliest spot in town with its restaurants and outdoor cafés, has been modernized and will soon boast a new casino as well.

The **Bastion,** refurbished under the supervision of Jean Cocteau, houses a museum containing a number of the master's works, such as the huge black and white mosaic entitled *The Salamander*, dated 1962, the important series of paintings of the *Lovers*, another of fantastic animals, and still another of portraits. Cocteau also frescoed the room in the local town hall, built in 1860 after the 17th-century Italian Classical style, in which civil weddings are held.

Menton, the port by night; the Bastion.

Menton, the Hôtel de Ville; the Church of Saint-Michel, in the old city.

The Old City of Menton

The façade of Saint-Michel; a charming view of the old city; panorama of the gulf.

This is one of the nicest places to wander about in. A stroll up and down old Menton's picturesque little streets offers charming views at every step. Off **Rue Longue,** the main thoroughfare of the city in the 17th century but still very much alive today, is a monumental staircase leading to the **Church of Saint-Michel.** On its mosaic pavement is the heraldic coat of arms of the Grimaldi family. The churchyard makes a delightful setting for the concerts of the International Chamber Music Festival. Built between 1619 and 1653 by Prince Honoré II of Monaco, the Church of Saint Michel was consecrated in 1675. Its charming Baroque façade is flanked by bell-towers. The interior, with a nave and two aisles, contains an admirable altarpiece by Antonio Manchello (1565) in the choir. The painting shows Saints Michael, Peter, and John the Baptist. The 18th-century wooden statue of St. Michael above the main altar is also of considerable note. In the Treasury, one of the outstanding pieces is a processional cross, the staff of which is actually a Turkish spear, part of the booty won by Prince Honoré I of Monaco in the Battle of Lépanto (1571) in which the Christian armies defeated the Turks.

Also in the churchyard is the **Chapelle des Pénitents Blancs**, otherwise known as the **Chapelle de la Conception**, with a fine two-story Renaissance façade decorated with statuary. The aisleless interior, with its frescoed ceilings, contains fourteen grandiose statues of saints.

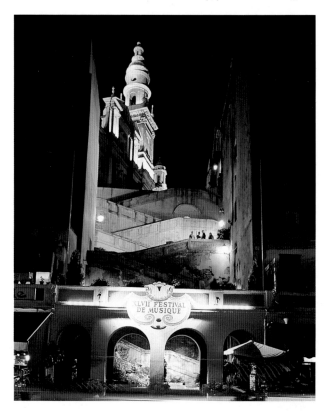

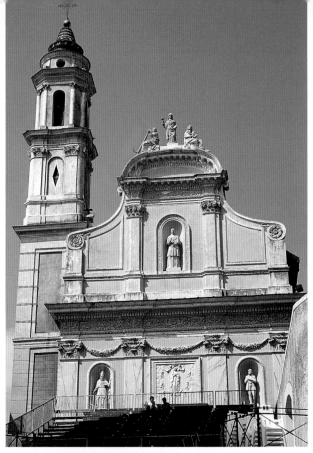

ROQUEBRUNE - CAP MARTIN

These enchanting resort towns are located along the coast between Menton and Monaco. Cap Martin, with its luxurious buildings on the sea, is the complete opposite of Roquebrune, an old village perched, together with its castle, atop the cliffs. The landscape consists of winding coastline alternating with craggy promontories covered with thick groves of pine and olive trees.

The Cap Martin Promontory

This beach resort is mainly a luxurious setting for the vacations of the very rich. A panoramic road overlooking the sea winds along the cliff's edge on the east side of the cape and passes beneath a Roman triumphal arch.

The Roquebrune Castle

The castle of Roquebrune is unique in all France, as it is the only Carolingian castle - and thus forerunner of the majestic feudal castles later built throughout the country - still standing. It was built by Conrad I of Ventimiglia in about 970 A.D. in order to defend his property from the Saracen invaders. Rising upon a cliff, the castle dominates the medieval village below. Its sturdy walls, ranging in thickness from three to twelve feet, are marked by the typically medieval arrow slits and embrasures and battlements with their merlons and crenelles. On the second floor is the ceremonial hall of feudal times, with the throne dating from the Middle Ages. The prison, with a cube-shaped cistern in the middle, is another interesting

View of Cap Martin.

The medieval hamlet of Roquebrune as seen from the castle; in the background, the Cap Martin promontory.

Roquebrune, the Carolingian castle that dominates the town; interior view of the castle; the courtyard of the stronghold from the fourth-floor lookout.

feature. On the third floor are more prison cells, the archers' dormitory, and the guard room. The fourth floor was set aside for the royal apartments. The terrace on the top floor commands a superb view which takes in Cap Martin, the Principality of Monaco, and Mont Agel.

The Town of Roquebrune

Roquebrune includes both the town and the castle, originally both enclosed within the same walls. The charming village is still medieval in appearance; its tiny streets are covered with Romanesque vaulting over steep slopes or ramps of stairs. Each year, the town provides the setting for three traditional processions: the Procession of the Dead Christ, re-enacting the burial of the Savior, held on the night of Good Friday; the Procession of the Limaces, held on the night of the Thursday following Corpus Domini; and the Procession of the Passion, first held in thanksgiving for the cessation of the 1467 plague epidemic and re-enacted on August 5th. The annual Broomflower Festival is held on June 21st. According to legend, these gay little yellow flowers kept the village, tempted by a perilous Siren, from plunging into the sea.

Suggestive views of the town of Roquebrune.

THE PRINCIPALITY OF MONACO
MONTE-CARLO

A Brief Historical Outline

The area we now call the Principality of Monaco was settled in the prehistoric era. Proof of the existence of these settlements are the rock-hewn refuges discovered near the Oceanographic Museum. Tradition has it that the area was inhabited by the Phoenicians, who built there a temple dedicated to Melkart, god of Tyre, later identified with the Greek god Heracles, also called Monoikos (the One). The Romans thus named the region Portulis Herculis Monoeci, from which derives the name Monaco. Julius Caesar set sail from this port on his way back to Rome to fight Pompeius. The Goths, Longobards, and Saracens later sacked and looted Monaco. The Republic of Genoa enfeoffed it in 1162, took it over in 1191, and erected a fortress there in 1215. At that point, a certain Francesco Grimaldi, nicknamed "Malizia" ("the Cunning"), a Guelph driven from Genoa, set out to conquer the fortress. Together with several of his followers, he managed to penetrate its walls disguised in a Franciscan habit, but he was unable to wrest control of it from its staunch defenders. Nonetheless, Charles II d'Anjou, Count of Provence, granted the castles of Villeneuve, Vence, and Cagnes to Ranier I Grimaldi (1267-1314), who was also appointed Admiral of France. The Grimaldi family coat of arms, supported by two monks brandishing swords, recalls Francesco's exploit. Finally, the principality fell to Charles I Grimaldi, also Admiral of France (d. 1358), whom Genoa recognized as sovereign of Monaco, Roquebrune, and Menton. After another series of ups and downs (under Ranier II, Jean I, Lambert, and Lucien), Honoré II (1604-1662) signed the Treaty of Péronne with Louis XIII, whereby Monaco became a French protectorate. Honoré was made Duke of Valentinois, Marquis of Baux, and Peer of France. Antoine I (1701-1731), lacking a male heir, gave his eldest daughter, Louise-Hippolyte, in marriage to Jacques Goyen de Matignon. De Matignon took the name and coat of arms of the Grimaldi family, and it is his descendants who presently rule Monaco. Following the French Revolution, the three cities of the principality joined together to form a republic and asked to be annexed to France (1792). In 1793 Monaco returned to its ancient name of Port-Hercules until in 1814 the Grimaldi family was restored as the ruling family. Nevertheless, the legitimate ruler Honoré preferred Paris and he never lived in Monaco at all. His successor, Florestan I, relinquished Menton and Roquebrune, which then proclaimed themselves free cities. When Charles III rose to the throne, the income from Monaco's taxes was practically nil, but instead of levying new heavy taxes on the population he instead had the idea of opening a special place where people could gamble, which would later became the Casino. Thus was created the Société des Bains de Mer; the year was 1861. Charles' idea proved a resounding success. The principality, now the gambling capital of Europe, rose from 3,000 to more than 15,000 inhabi-

tants in the span of just thirty years. In fact, the situation proved so advantageous that Charles decided to abolish direct taxation in Monaco completely. Nowadays the Société des Bains de Mer owns the Casino, the Sporting Club, the bathing establishments and the Mont Agel Golf Club. Following the death of Charles III, his son Albert I, a famed oceanographer, came to the throne. Albert gave the citizens of Monaco a new constitution based upon the electoral system. When he died in 1922, his son and successor Louis II made further improvements to the promenade, creating the Larvotto and the Monte-Carlo Beach. Louis was succeeded in May of 1949 by his grandson Ranier III, who had fought in the French army between 1944 and 1945. In 1956 Ranier wed the American movie star Grace Kelly. An economic boom and period of intensive real estate development followed. Taking advantage of the extremely liberal tax laws then in effect in Monaco, numerous foreign firms set up their headquarters in the country. The situation was such that France was forced to step in, and on May 18, 1963, the signing of new agreements considerably curbed tax advantages to foreigners.

Monaco, the Palace of the Princes; their Serene Highnesses Prince Ranier III and Crown Prince Albert.

Economic Resources

The main resource of Monaco is by far tourism. Everything here is created to delight the tourist, from the ultra-modern hotel complexes to Larvotto's man-made beach, the Sporting Club, and many many more. This is all topped by a year-round season including every kind of special event, highlighted by the renowned Rally of Monte-Carlo and the Grand Prix of Monaco car races, the International Festival of the Arts, the Gala Ball put on by Monaco's Red Cross, the International Circus Festival, the Gala de la Rose, and a host of others. But Monaco also boasts flourishing industrial resources: its food, chemical, mechanical, clothing, and construction industries are of no small note. In order to exploit its limited territory to the utmost, Monaco has set out on a far-reaching program of modernization and development, mainly aimed at reclaiming land from the sea with the embankments of Portier, Larvotto, and Fontvieille.

Government

Monaco is governed by a constitutional monarchy, with executive power held by the ruling Prince. The government is composed of a Minister of State, and three government advisors, all of whom are appointed by the Prince. The parliament is made up of eighteen members elected every five years by direct universal balloting.

Monaco, the Place d'Armes of the Palace of the Princes at the changing of the guard; the Place d'Armes in a painting by Joseph Bressan (1732).

Customs, Post Office and Currency

As far as customs are concerned, the frontiers with France are fully open. The principality issues its own stamps, even though the postal service is handled by the French. It also has its own currency, which is minted at the Hotel des Monnaies in Paris. French currency, however, is welcome everywhere.

SIGHTSEEING IN THE PRINCIPALITY

The main tourist attractions in Monaco are Le Rocher and its palace, old Monaco, and Monte-Carlo and the Larvotto complex.

The Palace

From the Place d'Armes at the foot of Le Rocher, an enormous ramp leads to the huge square (decorated with cannons donated by Louis XIV) on which the palace rises. The changing of the guard at the main palace entrance, every day at 11:55 am, is a fascinating sight.

Monaco, the monumental staircase of the courtyard of the Palace of the Princes; the Place d'Armes with the cannons donated by Louis XIV.

Monaco, the façade of the palatine chapel of Saint Jean-Baptiste, in the Palace courtyard; the Galerie d'Hercule, decorated with frescoes and grotesques in Renaissance style, in the Palace of the Princes.

Monaco, the throne-room of the Palace of the Princes.

The Grimaldi family as depicted by Ralph Wolfe Cowan.

The palace was originally a fortress, begun by Fulvo di Castello in 1215 for the Republic of Genoa. The only part of the fortress still standing is the Serravalle Tower on the west side and the eastern parapet, with its three crenelated towers. In the 19th century, Honoré II decided to make the fortress into a palace, transforming the whole interior without sacrificing the defensive elements. Louis I commissioned the portal surmounted by the Grimaldi coat of arms (1672). The building, with its two-story loggias, was erected in the late 16th century, while the chapel in the west wing dates to 1656.
During the French Revolution, the palace was turned into a military hospital and was sacked. In 1894, Prince Albert I commissioned the construction of the **Tour de l'Horloge** (Clocktower). Finally, Ranier III had the southern wing (destroyed during the French Revolution) completely rebuilt.

Monaco, Palace of the Princes: the Mazarin Room with its 17th-century boiserie and the portrait of Princess Grace painted by Ricardo Macaron in 1974; the hall of Louis XV.

Gilded-wood Louis XV furniture in the Blue Room of the Palace of the Princes; in the Mazarin Room, a chest with boiserie representing Hercules and the Hydra of Lerna.

The first thing that strikes your eye as you enter the palace is its magnificent courtyard, surrounded by arcades the vaults of which are decorated with 16th- and 17th-century frescoes. A superb double marble staircase leads to the **Galerie d'Hercule** (1552), decorated with frescoes depicting the Labors of Hercules, by Orazio Ferrari. At the end of the courtyard is the **Chapelle de St. Jean-Baptiste**, built in 1656 and restored in the 19th century. The medallions on the façade, painted in 1874 by Froschle and Deschler of Augsburg, show scenes from the life of St. Dévote and the main events in Monegasque history.

The **Musée Napoléonien et des Archives** is situated in the south-west wing of the palace. Prince Louis II was the first to take up collecting Napoleonic relics (the Grimaldi family is related to the Bonapartes). Prince Ranier III continued in his footsteps and set up the museum to display the collection, which contains many fascinating mementos pertaining to Napoleon, the man and the Emperor. The collection totals over one thousand objects and documents.

The Cathedral

The Romanesque-style cathedral, built of white stone from La Turbie, was erected on the site of the 13th-century church of St. Nicholas, demolished in 1874.

The church, with a nave and two aisles, is built on the Latin cross plan. There is a chapel on either side of the choir: on the left, the princes' funeral chapel (where Monaco's royal princes have received burial since 1505) and on the right the **Chapelle du Sacré-Coeur** with a 16th-century sculpted wooden altar. At the right of the transept we note a fine altarpiece dedicated to St. Nicholas, sculpted by Louis Bréa in 1500. The same artist is responsible for the superb *Pietà du Curé Teste* (1505) over the door to the sacristy. At the sides are panels representing St. Stephen and St. James the Greater (School of Nice, 16th century). To the right, in the deambulatory of the apse, is a processional canopy called the "*dais de Charles-Quint*". In the chapel of the apse is a *Pietà* by François Bréa, which has undergone considerable restoration. In the dome of the apse is Fachina's Byzantine-style mosaic of the *Immaculate Conception* (1886).

Monaco, Palace of the Princes: the York chamber, where the brother of King George II of England died on 14 September 1776.

Monaco, the Cathedral in Romanesque style, built between 1875 and 1903.

National Museum of Monaco

The delightful collection of old fashioned dolls and movable toys (*Automates et poupées d'autrefois*) was put together by Madeleine de Galea and donated to the Principality by her grandson. The museum building is actually a fine 19th-century villa designed by Charles Garnier. Before the building is a superb rose garden; a delightful array of delicately-colored flowers enthralls the eye. The garden contains many sculptures, including the famous *Jeune Faune* (Young Faun) by Carpeaux. Inside, the automatons are beautifully displayed in glass showcases. These amazing little figures, all in working order, come from the most renowned factories such as Vichy, Phalibois, Lambert, Decamps, Triboulet, and Renoux. The collection boasts a unique piece known as *Le Peintre-poète* (The Painter-Poet). There is also an extraordinary Neapolitan crèche containing over 250 figurines, and a collection of Provençal crèche statuettes.

The Exotic Garden

The garden, situated on a cliff overlooking the Fontvieille area, was masterfully laid out by the renowned landscape architect Louis Notari. The terraces afford stupendous panoramas of Le Rocher of Monaco, the harbor, Monte-Carlo, Cap Martin and Cap Ferrat. Stairs cut into the living rock, foot-bridges and paved lanes wind through the exuberant vegetation that often takes bizarre shapes typical of the tropical plants: cacti defended by their myriad thorns, other succulents, Euphorbiaceae, and the like. There is also an outstanding collection of arborescent cacti, some of which stand almost 20 feet tall!

The National Museum of Monaco, designed by Charles Garnier in the late 19th century.

Some of the splendid automatons in the Decamps collection, in the National Museum of Monaco: the Snake Charmer *(Paris, 1889) and the* Dining-Hall, *mechanical dolls from 1885.*

Monaco, views of the Exotic Garden with examples of rare plants.

Examples of Mexican cacti (Echinocactus grusani) almost 150 years old.

The Observatory Grottos

The grottos opening onto the Exotic Garden should not be overlooked. 250 steps lead down into the grotto cave, but the effort of descending them (and then climbing up again!) is well worth the trouble. The stalactites, stalagmites, and the other oddly-shaped formations create a fairytale-like setting of extravagant forms that recall the work of a surrealist painter. The grottos are important remains of the Quaternary era.

Museum of Prehistoric Anthropology

This museum was founded in 1904 by Albert I, the oceanographer-prince. It contains the collection of prehistoric objects and fossils discovered in the excavations at the Rochers Rouges, near Menton, as well as remains of the Grimaldi Negroid and Cro-Magnon man from the Paleolithic and Neolithic periods found in the grottos in Monaco's Exotic Garden. The museum also possesses an important collection of antique coins and gold jewelry and a collection of objects discovered in ancient Chilean tombs.

Fossilized remains of the Cro-Magnon man of the Grimaldi grotto.

A suggestive image of the grottos opening on the Exotic Garden.

The Oceanographic Museum of Monaco, inaugurated by Prince Albert I in 1911; the Hall of Marine Zoology with skeletons of the great sea mammals.

Oceanographic Museum

The museum, housed in a monumental building designed by Delafortrie and built right into a cliff over the water, was inaugurated in 1911. The initiative was promoted by Prince Albert I. An aficionado of the sea and underwater exploration, a pioneer in oceanography, a member of the Academy of Science, and founder of the Oceanographic Institute of Paris, he founded this museum to house the collections he had put together during the course of his explorations. Attached to the museum there is also a research institute with laboratories open to local and foreign scientists.

The Main Hall contains an exhibit of the equipment required for underwater exploration. The eighty tanks in the Aquarium, kept filled with sea water by means of pumps, contain strange specimens of fish and sea animals and the most unusual kinds of marine flora.

The Hall of Mammals contains the skeletons of the largest of the marine mammals, such as whales, narwhals, killer whales, etc., as well as a great many embalmed specimens. There are also numerous examples of the marine fauna discovered by Albert I on his scientific expeditions.

MONTE-CARLO

Monte-Carlo is the very symbol of luxurious living and all the earthly pleasures that money can buy. It also conjures up visions of Lady Luck, as the sky-high bets placed at the Casino bear out. Here all is organized for non-stop pleasure-making and the well-being of those rich enough to afford it. The origins of this incredible city lie in the economic hardships suffered by Charles III, Prince of Monaco, whose tiny country was gravely lacking in natural and other resources. Agriculture was poorly developed and at that time no industry existed to offset this defect. But Charles got the idea of promoting tourism and decided he could attract large numbers of people by building a gambling establishment and turning his kingdom into a permanent resort. After a somewhat half-hearted and hardly profitable attempt at opening a gaming-house himself, he had the good sense to turn the project over to an expert, François Blanc, who proceeded to found the Société des Bains de Mer. The Casino was built, and its success was such that Charles III graciously exempted the city from direct taxation! The newly-founded city took on the Italianized name of its prince: Monte-Carlo. By now the floodgates were open: building projects, new designs, and new ideas burst forth. As time went by, ultramodern buildings, sports facilities, night-clubs and the like sprang up, and Monte-Carlo became the meeting-place for the wealthy from all over the world. Since Monaco is so incredibly tiny, the embankments of Portier and Larvotto were created, and with them the Sea Club, Monte-Carlo Beach, a magnificent bathing

Sketch for a water-color affiche touting Monte-Carlo night-life, by Jean Gabriel Domergue, ca. 1930.

Monte-Carlo, Promenade on the Terrace of the Casino in a painting by Lelong.

A suggestive view of Monaco by night.

establishment with a swimming pool, beach, and restaurants), the man-made beach of Larvotto and the Monte-Carlo Sporting Club. The latter, inaugurated in 1974, was built right on the Larvotto embankment. It is a wholly modern, luxurious complex which includes the "Salle des Étoiles," the gambling club, discothèques, outdoor movie theatres, and restaurants. A new four-story **Centre de Congrès** has recently been added. It is designed to handle a wide range of activities such as cultural events, conferences and meetings, concerts, theatrical events, etc.

Monte-Carlo, a view of the port; the roof of the Centre de Congrès, with a mosaic by Victor Vasarely (1979).

Monte-Carlo: a view of the Louis II stadium, home to prestigious international sports events; the Sporting Club of Monte-Carlo.

The Monte-Carlo Casino

The construction of the Casino was begun in 1878. It is actually composed of several structures: the oldest is the theater overlooking the sea (1878-1879), designed by Charles Garnier, the architect responsible for the Paris Opera House; the most recent building, designed by the architect Médicin and built in 1910, is noteworthy for its painted and sculpted turn-of-the-century decorative scheme. Besides the theater, the Casino contains a number of richly decorated gambling rooms. There are both public rooms, such as the Grand Salon de l'Europe, the Salon des Amériques and the Salon des Grâces, and private rooms such as the two Touzet Rooms and the huge Salle François Médicin. A monumental staircase leads to the Salon de Thé (Tea Room) and the night club.

The Monte-Carlo Casino: a roulette table; a view of the façade of the Casino, built by Charles Garnier in 1878.

In the entrance-way to the Casino stand the sculptures of Hector and Andromache by Giorgio De Chirico.

The François Médecin game-room in the Monte-Carlo Casino. Green-baize table; a roulette wheel.

The sumptuous Salle Garnier theater with the Princes' Box, completed in 1879; the box is surmounted by the painting by Feynen-Perrin, The Song of Eloquence, and sculptures by Jules Thomas.

The **Salle Garnier** theater has hosted many important performances, including Gabriel Fauré's Masques et Bergamasques and Maurice Ravel's *L'Enfant et les Sortilèges*, and some of the world's best known artists have graced its stage: Sarah Bernhardt, Enrico Caruso, Anna Pavlova and others. The Russian Ballet, directed by Sergei Diaghilev, has given more than one hundred performances here, among which the celebrated *Spectre de la Rose* danced by Serge Lifar. Nijinskij, Leonid Massine, Yvette Chauviré and many others have also danced in the Salle Garnier. Opera activity flourishes; the house orchestra is world-renowned and the most prestigious directors in the world have stood on the theatre's podium.

Place du Casino

This square is one in a series of stupendous gardens with many flower beds and spacious paths criss-crossing palm-shaded lawns. In the square dominated by the façade of the Casino we also note the celebrated **Hôtel de Paris,** a typically Napoleon III style building. It was completely refurbished and modernized in order to achieve the utmost in functionality (for instance, the rooms are all air-conditioned), but its Belle Epoque character has been scrupulously respected. The appeal of its luxurious atmosphere and comfort is thus enhanced by the feeling of an epoch that was perhaps less anxiety-ridden than ours.

Night-time view of the entrance to the Monte-Carlo Casino; the façade of the Casino, facing the sea.

La Turbie, the remains of the imposing Trophée des Alpes; reconstruction of the monument.

Details of the Trophée des Alpes.

A view of La Turbie.

LA TURBIE

The origins of La Turbie may be traced back to the 10th century. Remains of the medieval period include the 11th- and 12th-century walls and a fortified harbor. The Baroque style church, dating back to 1777, contains a number of fine paintings as well as a noteworthy onyx and agate table (in the choir).

Trophée des Alpes

At the time of Caesar's death, some tribes were still in revolt, but his successor Augustus succeeded in quelling the rebellion. In the year 6 B.C. the Senate and Romans decided to erect a triumphal arch to commemorate this victory. *Le Trophée des Alpes* (or *Tour d'Auguste*) must have originally stood 164 meters tall over a base measuring over 124 meters along each side. Over the years it fell into disrepair but it has recently been restored.

EZE

Perched like an eagle's nest on a craggy peak, Eze has preserved its unique medieval appearance with tiny streets covered over by vaults and ancient buildings packed closely together.

Its name derives from a Phoenician temple dedicated to Isis. Beneath one of the vaults is the **Chapelle des Pénitents Blancs** built in 1036 and restored in 1954. Eze also has a very attractive Exotic Garden.

Eze, the clock-tower; a suggestive view of the medieval hamlet.

Besides its beaches and the charm of the old section of town, Eze also boasts an interesting exotic garden.

BEAULIEU-SUR-MER

One of the most interesting sights in this resort town is the **Villa Kérylos**, located on the panoramic Pointe des Fourmis. Built by the architect Emanuele Pontremoli for the archeologist Theodor Reinach (d. 1928), the building is a faithful reproduction of a Greek villa of antiquity. All the elements are based on authentic antique pieces and only the finest materials were used in its construction: marble from Carrara, Siena, and Serravezza (the latter variety is known as "peach blossom"), exotic woods for the furniture, and the like. The many authentic pieces preserved inside the villa only add to its appeal: it is a true masterpiece.

The beach at Beaulieu-sur-Mer.

The Villa Kerylos at Pointe des Fourmis; views of the splendid villa, built for the archeologist Theodor Reinach.

The magnificent garden of the Ile-de-France villa and museum at Saint-Jean Cap Ferrat.

The park of the villa of Saint-Jean is studded with tropical plants and rare aromatic herbs; the interior of the villa is richly furnished and exhibits the beautiful porcelains of Sèvres and Saxe.

SAINT-JEAN CAP FERRAT

Saint-Jean is an old fishing village which has become a luxury residential area. Its location is superb; here the coast is rocky and covered by thick groves of pines. The **Villa-Musée Ile-de France** (the Ephrussi de Rothschild Foundation), with its magnificent museum, is an unfailing draw for sightseers.

Villa-Musée Ile-de-France

Founded by Béatrice Ephrussi de Rothschild, the villa is surrounded by a splendid garden fragrant with the scent of rare aromatic herbs and tropical plants and decorated with statues, pools, and even a copy of the *Temple de l'Amour*, the original of which stands in the Trianon of Versailles. Inside there are furnishings of the Regency, Louis XV, and Louis XVI periods, Savonnerie rugs, and Beauvais and Aubusson tapestries. The frescoes on the ceilings are by Tiepolo, Coypel, and Pellegrini. There are also statues by Falconnet, paintings and drawings by Boucher, Fragonard, Gustave Moreau, and Hubert Robert, as well as Impressionist works by Sisley, Monet, and Renoir. In addition, there is a fine collection of Sèvres and Saxe porcelain and Clodion pottery.

VILLEFRANCHE-SUR-MER

The harbor of Villefranche is renowned for its beauty: one and a quarter miles in length and two-thirds of a mile wide, it could probably contain a whole naval squadron - and in fact, it was the military port of the Sardinian kings. The **old city**, shaped like an amphitheater, has preserved its original appearance. One of the streets, **Rue Obscure**, was so named because it is almost entirely covered over. In the tiny, picturesque port there are inscriptions to commemorate the visits of Charles V of Spain and Pope Paul III in 1538. The **fortress,** the bastions of which have been turned into gardens, was built by Emmanuel-Philibert of Savoy in the 16th century. The **Chapelle de Saint-Pierre,** frescoed by Jean Cocteau, is a worthwhile sight.

Two views of the port of Villefranche-sur-Mer.

The harbor of Villefranche, renowned for its beauty; panorama of the old city.

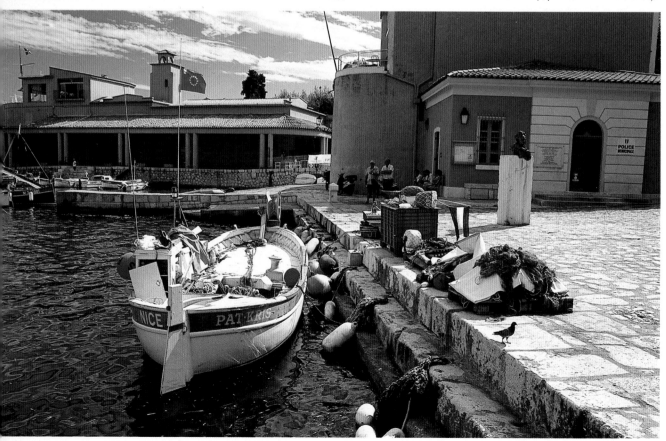

The fountain near the bastions of the Villefranche
fortress; the bastions raised by Emmanuel-Philibert of Savoy
in the 16th century.

The façade of the Chapelle de Saint-Pierre; a view of the old city;
Saint-Michel's Church.

The interior portico of the fortress.

Nice, view of the port and the bay.

NICE

Capital of the Côte d'Azur, Nice extends along the magnificent Baie des Anges (Bay of Angels). Owing to its extraordinary location, it has been inhabited since remote times: the Phoenicians, Ligurians, Greeks and Romans all settled it in various periods. After the population was converted to Christianity in about the 4th century, Nice alternated under the Provençal, Savoy, Italian and French flags until 1860, when it finally became definitively French. Today, Nice is one of the most renowned cities in France; foreigners come to see and enjoy it all year round. They particularly relish the comforts of a bustling modern city and the excitement of numerous cultural events which range from conferences to expositions, exhibits, festivals, and the like. Nevertheless, traditions such as the famous Nice carnival still live on and important mementos of the city's ancient past can still be found in the charming old section with its narrow streets, flower market, and ancient port. The name Nice immediately brings to mind the renowned **Promenade des Anglais**, which has come to stand for Nice itself and is a meeting-place for people from all over the world.

The "Promenade des Anglais"

The renowned Promenade des Anglais, which runs along the sea-side, was the brainstorm of a certain Reverend Lewis Way in 1822. He thought it would be an excellent idea to have this part of the coast leveled off, since he had noticed that his fellow Englishmen were especially fond of taking their strolls up and down this strip. The name Promenade des Anglais dates from 1844. Today the promenade is an elegant street lined with fashionable shops and celebrated buildings such as the **Hôtel Negresco** (memento of the Belle Epoque), the **Hôtel Royal**, the **Ruhl Casino**, and the **Palais de la Méditerranée**.

The port

The port was built by Charles Emmanuel III, Duke of Savoy. Begun in 1750, it was soon dubbed "Port Lympia" (port of the clear waters). Daily ferries bound for Corsica sail from its four docks. There are numerous restaurants along the quays which do much to enliven the atmosphere. The brightly colored houses and the parish church add to the charm of the lovely scene.

Nice, sunset over the bay; the celebrated "Promenade des Anglais"; in the background, the Hôtel Negresco.

Nice, the Chapelle de la Miséricorde ou des Pénitents Noirs; the flower market; the cathedral of Ste. Réparate.

The Old City

No one should fail to visit the old city. It is like taking a sudden plunge into the past - here the buildings that line the narrow streets all date back to the 17th or 18th centuries. Take a closer look around: doesn't this remind you of some other city? Of course, that's it - Venice. And, as a matter of fact, in Nice you can find the same little squares, the paved alleyways, the flower pots at the windows, and laundry hanging out to dry on the balconies. Many of the streets are literally lined with shops, where craftsmen work the very same way that their predecessors of one hundred years ago did - practically outside on the street. Even the little cafés have their tables set up outdoors, right on the street, since there is no room for sidewalks. It would seem that not even the sun dare peek in here - you encounter it only at street-corners or squares, when you emerge from the cool shadowy recesses of the tunnel-like streets. Don't miss visiting the **Church of St. François de Paule** (by Guaring, 1733-1750), the **Chapelle de la Miséricorde ou des Pénitents Noirs** (Bernardo Vittone's Baroque masterpiece of 1736), the **Cathedral of Ste. Réparate** (by J. A. Duibera, 1650), and lastly, the **Palais Lascaris.**

The Flower Market

The flower market is located in the heart of the old section of the city; with its lively atmosphere and colorful arrays of plants and flowers it is one of the most pleasurable experiences the old city offers the tourist.

Palais Lascaris

Located in the old city, the palace was originally the home of the Lascaris-Vintimille family. It was built in the 17th century after the Genoese style and remodelled and redecorated in the 18th century. The latest restoration work dates to 1963. The building is four stories tall, with decorative elements adorning the façade at the first- and second-floor levels. On the ceiling of the vestibule are painted the family's coat of arms and motto (*Nec me fulgura*: "the same thunderbolt shall not slay me"). This decoration dates from the 17th century, whereas the statuary and niches were added a century later. The decoration of the second floor ceilings, frescoes of mythological scenes, is attributed to Giovanni Battista Carlone (c. 1670). The **Pharmacie** downstairs contains a fine collection of 18th-century ceramic apothecary jars. There is also a collection of old musical instruments on permanent display. Flemish tapestries showing scenes from the life of Achilles decorate the walls.

Nice, Palais Lascaris: detail of the indoor staircase decorated with statues, niches and grotesques; the beautiful collection of apothecary jars exhibited in the palace.

Nice, the fountains in Place Masséna; the celebrated rose trellises.

Place Masséna, the monument to Albert I of Belgium; a modern sculpture and, in the background, the Ruhl Casino; plays of water in Place Masséna.

Place Masséna

At the heart of the city, Place Masséna is constantly trafficked, since it the convergence point of all the city's main thoroughfares. On one side of the square is a charming park, called the Jardin Albert Ier, with arched rose trellises pleasantly shading the pathways. On the other side, the ochre-colored buildings with porticos lend a Genoese air. Leading off the square is Rue Masséna, the center of Nice's night life and one of the many streets in the city's delightful pedestrian zone.

The entrance to the Musée Masséna; one of the halls in the museum embellished with frescoes, period furniture and gilded wood decoration; the Room of Armor.

Musée Masséna

The museum was built at the turn of the century. The ground floor, used for the official ceremonies organized by the city of Nice, is beautifully furnished in Empire style. The rest of the museum is dedicated to local history and includes exhibits of the primitive and sacred art of the region.

The Russian Orthodox Cathedral

This striking five-domed cathedral was designed by the architect Préobrajensky and erected between 1903 and 1912. It contains frescoes painted by Designori and a number of fine icons, among which a copy of the *Divine Savior* from the Cathedral of the Assumption in Moscow.

View of the Russian Orthodox Cathedral and the magnificent chapel built in 1868 in memory of Zarevich Nicholas, son of Alexander II of Russia with The Presentation of the Virgin at the Temple *at its center.*

Nice, the interior of the former Russian Orthodox church in Rue Longchamp, built in 1859.

The spectacular man-made waterfall of the Nice castle; the Bellanda Tower, at the summit of the Nice castle.

Nice, Naval Museum: the huge painting by Gudin depicting the arrival of Napoleon II in Genoa.

Detail of the mosaics in the castle garden.

The Castle Waterfall

The castle's man-made cascade falls from the highest point in Nice (302 feet). From its summit you can enjoy an unforgettable view of the city below.

The Castle

Of the old fortress, razed to the ground in 1706, there remain only traces today. The site has instead been converted to a delightful park shaded by pines, a lovely setting for a stroll.

The Beach

Even though Nice's beach is gravel and not fine sand, it is always crowded, since it is one of the best equipped in all of Europe. The beach also boasts numerous restaurants and terraces that offer a magnificent panorama of the Baie des Anges.

Views of the Nice's famous (and crowded) beaches.

Nice, the beautiful façade of the Musée Jules Chéret.

Paul Signac, Le pont des Saints-Pères.

Musée Chéret

One of the typically opulent Belle Epoque mansions in Nice, the museum building is in pure Piedmontese Baroque style despite the fact that it was built in the late l9th century (1878). Originally property of a Russian princess, Mme. Kotschoubey, it was bought by the City of Nice in 1928. Most of the funds were put up by private citizens, among whom the founder of the museum, Jules Chéret (1863-1932), painter and poster artist, Baron Joseph Vitta, the widows of painters Mossa and Dufy, and Pablo Picasso, who in 1955 made a donation of thirteen ceramics. The collection, including works from different periods and schools, provides an excellent panorama of four centuries of European art (17th through 20th).

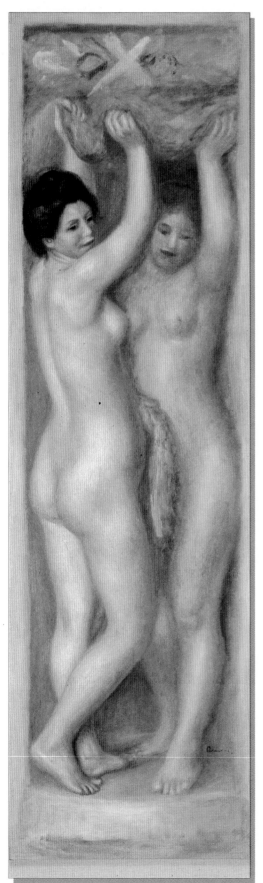

Pierre-Auguste Renoir, Les grandes baigneuses.

Pierre-Auguste Renoir, Les cariatides.

Carl van Loo, Neptune et Amymone.

Musée National "Message Biblique" de Marc Chagall

This building was designed for the sole purpose of showing off Marc Chagall's *Le Message Biblique* (The Biblical Message). The architect was André Hermant. "My intention was not to portray the dream of a single people, but rather to represent the dream of all humanity," said Chagall referring to this series of seventeen enormous panels. His is a true message of love: "In art, just as in life, everything is possible provided that at the base there is Love," he went on to say. These panels depict scenes which are familiar to our spirit, aglow with Chagall's striking palette of blues against greens, highlighted with a dash of red or purple which makes them almost sing out; the figures, likewise familiar, in turn unreal and strikingly vivid, fly about in space, unhampered by the earthly laws of gravity. The 17 panels that make up the Biblical Message proper are enhanced by a mosaic of the *Prophet Elijah on the Chariot of Fire*, three sculptures (*Moses, David,* and *Christ Crucified*), and an immense stained glass window *(The Creation of the World)* by Chagall and Franz Marc. The museum also contains the artist's 250 preparatory sketches, as well as gouaches, engravings, and lithographs.

Marc Chagall, Elijah on the Chariot of Fire, *mosaic.*

Marc Chagall and Franz Marc, the windows of the auditorium.

Marc Chagall, Abraham and the Three Angels.

Harpsichord decorated by Chagall.

Following pages: splendid panoramic view of Nice by night.

The famous Hôtel Negresco on the "Promenade des Anglais" in Nice; the sumptuous decoration of the hall of the Hôtel, one of the most renowned in the world.

Hôtel Negresco

The most celebrated building along the Promenade is the Hôtel Negresco, declared a French landmark in 1974. It was built by a Rumanian businessman-violinist, Henry Negresco, in 1912 for a select clientele composed mainly of aristocrats and the extremely well-to-do. Edward Niermans, the Dutch architect who designed it, did not stray from the taste of his times. The result is an imposing, somewhat overelaborate structure - in short, a building that can be described as anything but austere. Although dozens of hotels affected by the worldwide economic crisis of the thirties were forced to close down, the Negresco managed to emerge virtually unscathed. The interior testifies to its well-preserved turn of the century opulence; the rooms are lavishly appointed with antique furnishings, thick velvets and carpeting, and elaborate stucco decoration.

The Ruhl Casino

Also on the busy Promenade des Anglais is the celebrated **Ruhl Casino**, an impressive modern ten-story building in the "New Nice" style, home as well to the rooms of the luxurious Hôtel Meridien.
The bets at the tables of the Ruhl are on a par with those of Monte-Carlo, and it is not rare to see entire fortunes laid on the baize.
The crowded halls of the Casino host many shows and concerts, making the Ruhl a sort of Moulin Rouge on the Côte d'Azur patronized by habitués from all over the world.

Another famous spot in Nice: the Ruhl Casino; a roulette; a show at the Ruhl.

CIMIEZ

In about 13 B.C., the Romans chose the ancient Celtic settlement of Cemenelum as the headquarters of their Alpes-Maritimes military detachment, in defense of the Via Julia-Augusta that led to Spain. 19th-century excavations brought to light a number of necropoli which were later earthed-in again. The **Parc des Arènes** contains vestiges of the ancient Roman city, including the amphitheater and the baths.

The Amphitheater

As amphitheaters go, this one is rather small (221.4 x 183.7 feet). By the time the city was founded in the 1st century A.D., the arena and five rows of seats had already been completed. The construction was enlarged in the 3rd century to hold up to 4,000 spectators. It was used for various events such as spear matches and gladiator contests, but not for animal combats.

The Baths

The baths were constructed between the 2nd and 3rd centuries A.D. Several of the buildings are still in an excellent state of preservation. The complex contained a *frigidarium* (cold room), a *tepidarium*, and two *calidaria*, a pool and other tubs. The cold room, located in the north section, is almost perfectly preserved. Almost 33 feet in height, for many centuries it was thought to be a temple of Apollo.

The façade of the Church of Notre-Dame in Nice.

Cimiez, the archaeological site.

Three masterpieces by Henri Matisse: Odalisque, Still Life with Books *and* Woman with Book.

Villa des Arènes

This edifice takes in two totally different museums, the **Musée Matisse** and the **Musée d'Archéologie**.

Musée Matisse

Even though Henri Matisse's major works are preserved elsewhere, the paintings and drawings on display here allow us to follow his evolution from the copies he made of the old masters up to his preparatory sketches for the Chapel of Vence. Of especial note are the *Still-Life with Harmonica* (1900), the *Odalisque with Red Box* (1926), the *Rocaille Armchair* (1946), and the *Still-Life with Pomegranates* (1947). Among the fine guaches is the *Creole Dancer* of 1950. There is also a fine collection of drawings and lithographs which reveal the artist's ever-present efforts to achieve greater and greater rigor. Lastly, the museum houses a number of personal objects used by the painter, a portrait of him painted by Derain, and a portrait of the artist's wife by Marquet.

Musée d'Archéologie

Created in 1960, the museum houses a collection of objects brought to light by the excavations at Cimiez, such as ceramics, Roman jewelry and pottery, and Greek, Etruscan, and Italic vases. Displays also illustrate life in the Cimiez of long ago.

Cimiez, the façade of the Villa des Arènes, home of the Musée Matisse and the Musée d'Archeologie.

Attic red-figured krater (5th century BC).

The statue of Antonia.

Dancing Faun, a Greek bronze from the 1st century B.C. found in Cimiez in 1904.

Church and Monastery of Cimiez

On the parvis of the church there rises a **trefoil cross** (1477) on which is sculpted the crucified Angel that appeared to St. Francis of Assisi. The façade of the church (1850) is in a style known as "gothique troubadour", whereas the porch is from 1662. The two-lanterned bell-tower rises on a square base.

The **interior** contains a number of interesting works. The nave dates from the 14th or 15th century, while the two aisles are later additions. The ribbed vaults are decorated with frescoes painted by the Venetian artist Giacomelli in 1859, and depict scenes from the history of the Franciscan order.

The church also contains three major works by the Bréa brothers (School of Nice, 15th-16th centuries): the *Pietà of Cimiez* (1475), one of Louis Bréa's finest works, the *Crucifixion* (1512) by Louis Bréa, and the *Deposition* by Antoine Bréa (16th century).

The church of Cimiez with its trefoil cross; view of the church and monastery.

The interior of the church of Cimiez; detail of the main altar.

The elaborate, sculpted and gilded wood **altarpiece** is a magnificent Baroque creation dated 1663. In the center portion, the Virgin is flanked by two bas-reliefs of Saints Peter and Paul and two angels; statues of St. Anthony of Padua and St. Didace decorate the niches. This lovely **Monastery Garden** is now a public park. Above it, on a hill covered by cypresses and oak trees, there once stood the Oppidum Ligure, the original nucleus from which the town of Cimiez grew.

The splendid town of Saint-Paul-de-Vence.

Characteristic views of the medieval hamlet of
Saint-Paul-de-Vence.

SAINT-PAUL-DE-VENCE

You can't help being enchanted by the scene which greets your eyes when you arrive in Saint-Paul. Nestling between two valleys with slopes cloaked in orange trees, cypresses and cultivations of flowers, this charming village rising upon a rocky promontory has preserved intact all of its medieval appeal. It is encircled by the imposing walls built by François I between 1537 and 1547. We enter the city from the **Porte Royale** (13th century), and immediately lose our way in little winding streets lined with old stone buildings with flowers in every window and *ateliers d'art* (art dealers) or souvenir shops below. In one of the many lovely squares we can admire the famous **Grande-Fontaine** and its vaulted wash-house. We stop a moment before the renowned **Hôtel de la Colombe d'Or**, a preferred stopping-place for many famous personalities and a true museum, with its paintings by Bonnard, Vlaminck,

Utrillo, Braque, Matisse and others. Nearby is a fascinating museum of musical instruments, the earliest of which is dated 1750.

The Church

The church was built in the 13th century, although the vaulting was redone in the 1600s and the bell-tower was rebuilt in 1740. Interesting works by Guido Reni, Lebrun, and Tintoretto may be admired inside. In the **sacristy treasury** there are silver and gilded silver pieces, among which a *Black Virgin*, reliquaries, and the like. Saint-Paul attracts many artists, especially painters, and is a must for lovers of modern art since about a half a mile from the village is the headquarters of the renowned **Maeght Foundation**.

Saint-Paul: the Maeght Foundation, the "Giacometti courtyard" and the central building with its unique rain-water collectors.

The Maeght Foundation

The Foundation was set up by Aimé Maeght and his wife, the owners of an equally famous Parisian art gallery. Their museum at Saint-Paul is unique as an ambience in which to show off and compare modern masterpieces, since the setting seems made to order to bring out all their vigor and force. The Foundation was inaugurated in 1964 by André Malraux, who was later given a grandiose retrospective during the summer 1973 season.

The Building and its Setting

The complex as a whole was designed by the Spanish-American architect Joseph Lluis in conjunction with his American studio and two local architects. Rising on the top of a hill in the middle of a pine grove, it is composed of two buildings of white poured concrete and colored bricks. The architectural style, while reminiscent of that prevalent in Provence, is not specifically local. The wishes of Aimé Maeght that the natural landscape be respected have been fully complied with and the grading of the terrain has been retained, although the smooth slope has been interrupted by two retainer walls; the roof rainwater drains, designed to supply the pools, and the purifiers vaguely resemble the starched white caps nuns once wore.

A sculpture by Joan Miró.

A distinctive feature of the Foundation garden are the large pools that reflect works by the greatest masters of modern art; a fascinating mobile fountain by Pol Bury in the Foundation garden.

Miró's Fork *in the Foundation garden.*

A work by Alberto Giacometti on exhibit in the courtyard that has been given his name.

The poured concrete roofs are in the shape of quarter-cylinders and, in the words of the architect Sert, they serve to "trap light". The great glass walls provide perfect daylight illumination. Sunlight never shines directly into the rooms, each of which is lit differently in relation to the kinds of works on display. Outside, the many pools reflect the work of the artists who decorated the buildings, such as the mosaics by Chagall and Braque (among others). Sculpture and ceramics by Miró enhance the **Labyrinthe.** The two wings of the complex are joined together by the **Cour Giacometti**, reserved entirely for the sculptural creations of the great modern master. The pine woods are dotted with Calder's mobiles, Miró's *Fork* also stands here. A chapel dedicated to St. Bernard was built in memory of Maeght's son, Bernard. It is decorated with stained glass windows by Bazaine and Braque and a *Via Crucis* by Ubac.

Marc Chagall's canvases stand out among the works of the great
20th-century masters.

A view of one of the rooms in the Foundation complex.

The Foundation Collections

The best-known masters of 20th-century art are represented in the museum: Adam, Bonnard, Arp, Giacometti, Kandinsky, Léger, Matisse, Germaine Richier,
Bazaine, Chagall, Barbara Hepworth, Tal Coat, etc.
The younger generation is represented by Pol Bury,
Alan Davie, Dodeigne, Hantaii, Palazuelo, and Re-
beyrolle, among others. Every year the Foundation puts
on two large-scale shows which are important events
in the international art world. But the Foundation's activities do not stop here. Throughout the summer, con-
temporary music concerts, ballets, and poetry readings
are held in the Cour Giacometti. The Foundation also
puts out a quarterly publication, L'Ephémère, and
awards fellowships and prizes to encourage creativity
in the arts.

CAGNES-SUR-MER

Cagnes is actually composed of three sections; **Cros-de-Cagnes** (with the fishing port and beach), **Haut-de-Cagnes** (the old town), and, between the two, **Le Logis** (the modern city). The **Musée Renoir** is in this latter section.

Musée Renoir

Auguste Renoir (b. 1841, d. 1919) spent the last eleven years of his life on his property in Les Colettes, a six-acre plot overgrown with centuries-old olive trees. In this simple dwelling in which Renoir, then in his seventies, continued with his painting despite his poor health, have been collected mementos and personal objects used by the artist: his wheelchair, palettes, brushes, and easels. In addition, there are two of his paintings, two sanguines, and two of his sculptures. In the garden there is a bust of his wife in terracotta and a bronze of the *Baigneuse*.

Villa Renoir at Cagnes-sur-Mer: two interiors showing reconstructions of the places where the artist spent the last years of his life and the statue of the Baigneuse.

The typical pointus lining the Cros-de-Cagnes waterfront.

The famous "Hippodrome de la Côte d'Azur" at Cros-des-Cagnes.

CROS-DE-CAGNES

This enchanting resort (really a section of Cagnes) possesses a pretty little fishing port with boats of a special kind called *pointus*. The banks are lined with a host of fine restaurants. From the beach, the village climbs up a hill to the Plateau des Bréguières, where there extend the greenhouses for the cultivation of flowers, especially carnations and mimosa.

HAUT-DE-CAGNES

The old section of Cagnes is perched upon a hill. The town, surrounded by an old wall, is full of charming, steeply rising streets lined with medieval houses, which in many cases have been beautifully restored. The 13th-century walls still contain their original city gates, one of which, the **Porte d'Antibes**, is flanked by its original guardhouse, recently restored.

The Church of St. Pierre

Below the castle is this two-part church, half in the archaic Gothic style, half in the 17th-century style. The statuary and paintings date from the 17th and 18th centuries.

Château Grimaldi

The castle that dominates the village was originally a fortress, built in the 14th century after Robert d'Anjou donated Cagnes to Ranier I Grimaldi as a fief. It was remodelled in 1620 by Henri Grimaldi who transformed it into a magnificent castle.

The Château Grimaldi at Haut-de-Cagnes.

View of the interior courtyard of the Grimaldi castle.

Château Grimaldi, the splendid trompe-l'oeil ceiling by Carlone.
Modern art exhibited in the Château Grimaldi at Haut-de-Cagnes.

Some of the masterpieces exhibited in the Château Grimaldi.

The triangular-shaped inner court is surrounded by three stories of superimposed galleries. The ground floor is dedicated to Grimaldi family history. The second floor, with a fine *trompe-l'oeil* ceiling painted by Carlone the Genoese (1625), was used for receptions (the fresco represents the *Fall of Phaéton*). In the boudoir, once belonging to the Marquise Grimaldi, there are forty portraits of singers (Suzy Solidor Bequest) by famous painters such as Dufy, Kisling, Foujita, etc.

VILLENEUVE-LOUBET

Marina-Baie-des-Anges

Some love them, some can't stand them. The modern high-risers built around a port with 600 moorings are pyramid-shaped, terraced constructions designed to make the most of sun and the sea view.

Musée de l'Art Culinaire

This unusual museum is actually the birthplace of Auguste Escoffier (b. 1846 d. 1935), defined as "the king of chefs and the chef of kings". A Provençal kitchen, replete with every sort of cooking device and implement, has been reconstructed inside the house. The museum also boasts a vast collection of documents, books, photos, china, and silverware, not to mention a fabulous collection of over 15,000 menus, many of which are curiously illustrated and some of which date to as early as 1820.

Chocolates and sugar-plums exhibited at the Musée de l'Art Culinaire in Villeneuve-Loubet; reconstruction of a traditional kitchen.

The futuristic complex of Marina-Baie- des-Anges

View of the walls and castle of Antibes; boats at anchor in the port.

ANTIBES

The Phoenicians founded Antipolis, today's Antibes, in the 4th century B.C. Later, under the Romans, it enjoyed a long period of great prosperity, until the time when the city was raided and looted by barbarian pirates. Sacked again by Charles V of Spain in 1536, it was reconquered by Charles-Emmanuel of Savoy and later taken over by Henry IV. Vauban gave it walls so mighty that they even withstood the Austrians (who were nonetheless able to gain control of Fort-Carré). Most of these walls were torn down, seemingly for no good reason, in 1895. All that remains of them today is the lovely promenade along the Avenue de l'Amiral-de-Grasse. Luckily, however, Antibes has managed to preserve her old city, which for sheer charm has no equal: a wistful air of times gone by permeates its tiny streets with their charming names, such as Rue Saint-Esprit.

The Church

This church is actually the old cathedral. The Romanesque apse and transept are still intact, but the rest of the construction dates from the 17th century (with the exception of the square **tower-refuge**, actually the bell-tower, which was erected in the 12th century). In the interior are a fine pulpit and some noteworthy 17th-century altarpieces as well as the lovely Altarpiece of the Rosary, painted by a follower of Bréa in 1515.

Fort-Carré

Perched upon a rock, Fort-Carré was built at the end of the 16th century around a tower dated 1550.

Archaeological Museum

The museum is housed in the bastion of St. André, a fortified building designed by Vauban. The exhibits thousands of pieces, among which is an Etruscan relic of the 5th century B.C.

The Castle and the Grimaldi Museum

This was originally the site of the Roman encampment (castrum), later the Bishop's residence and still later the home of the Grimaldis, from 1385 to 1608. Though the present building dates from the 17th century, it was restored in 1830. The Museum Grimaldi contains a collection of Gallic-Roman pieces on the patio. In a small room inside is a fine altarpiece by Antoine Aundi: the *Swooning of the Virgin* (1529). On the terrace are sculptures by Germaine Richier.

Antibes: the ancient cathedral with its 17th-century façade and the fortified tower.

The imposing mass of the Antibes castle.

Antibes, the Picasso Museum: sculptures and ceramics by the master.

The Picasso Museum

The works displayed are mainly those Picasso painted on the spot, all of mythological and Mediterranean inspiration. The collection totals 23 paintings, 33 drawings, 78 ceramics, 2 sculptures, and 27 lithographs. The museum also contains works by other well-known modern masters such as Gastaud, Léger, Atlan, and Rouault.

Cannes, the crowded Boulevard de la Croisette.

CANNES

Cannes is probably the most elegant spot on the whole Côte d'Azur. Its magnificent bay, extending before the **Lérins Islands**, framed by mountains, its lovely sandy beaches, superb climate, and charming port all contribute to making it a truly unique vacation spot. Nature's gifts are enhanced by the luxurious villas, the gardens full of brightly colored flowers, the celebrated **La Croisette** and the many festivals. Actually, it was an Englishman, Lord Brougham, who brought fame and fortune to Cannes: prevented from entering Italy because of the cholera epidemic then raging in Provence (the year was 1834), he was forced to stop at Cannes and was so enthralled by its charm and climate that he decided to build himself a castle there. His presence drew other Englishmen, who were followed by many other foreigners, English and otherwise. Cannes' debt to Lord Brougham has been commemorated by a statue raised in his memory. The prosperity which derived from the ensuing building and general economic boom sparked construction of La Croisette, the renowned boulevard which runs for 1.5 miles along the seafront and is lined with famous buildings.

The manifold festivals, including the Flower Battle, the Mimosa Festival, and international boat races, draw great crowds every year. The city also hosts two other important yearly events: the Midem and the International Film Festival. But year round, festivals or not, Cannes is always the destination of a steady stream of cosmopolitan visitors: fashionably-clad foreigners, bejewelled grand dames, young lovelies out stalking fortune, and gamblers ... sometimes wondering where theirs went!

Boulevard de la Croisette

The Croisette is lined with any number of famous buildings which evoke memories of the distant and not so distant past - the **Hôtel Carlton,** the **Hôtel Royal**, the **Municipal Casino** in *Belle Epoque* style, the Roaring Twenties **Casino d'Été**, and the **Casino du Palm-Beach**; and, naturally, the **Palais des Festivals et des Congrès**, where all sorts of cultural events and conferences, including the Cannes International Film Festival, are held.
The magnificent Boulevard de la Croisette is also embellished by enchanting public parks with their palm trees and rare aromatic herbs.

The Casino of Cannes.

Cannes, the Palais des Festivals et des Congrès, where the golden palms for film excellence are awarded.

The fountains near the Palais des Festivals.

Film stars leave memories of themselves here as in Hollywood.

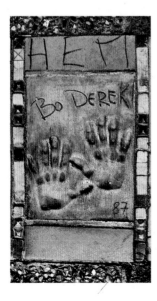

The Cannes Beach

This magnificent sandy beach is always packed and offers the most diverse and unusual attractions. Besides the public areas, there are several private bathing establishments, with a clientele among the most fashionable to be found anywhere.

The beach and the waterfront are among Cannes' main attractions.

The Lérins Islands

Studding the Gulf of Cannes are the small islands of Lérins, Sainte-Marguerite and Saint-Honorat, home to a fortified monastery and a Cistercian abbey dating to the 11th century. The thick stands of pines and eucalyptus host numerous protected species of animals.

View of the Lérins Islands.

Sunset over the port of Cannes.

Cannes, the old port by night; panoramic view of the port.

View of the port of Cannes.

The Port of Cannes

Cannes is an important tourist port. Hundreds of boats, often luxurious yachts, are anchored here year-round. Strolling along the Allées de la Liberté, lined with plane trees, you can see them moored at the docks. Going out on the quay provides a stupendous view of the hills of **Super-Cannes** and, at their feet, the **Boulevard de La Croisette** and its magnificent buildings. Charming, brightly colored houses line the promenade. And in the evening, when the little open-air restaurants are lit up and their lights reflect in the water, it looks as though the port is illuminated for some marvellous celebration.

Notre-Dame d'Espérance

This church is situated in the du Suquet district of the old city. Built between 1521 and 1648, in the "Southern Gothic" style, it contains some noteworthy works of art, among which altarpieces, reliquary busts dating from the 17th century, and two painted wood statues (one of St. Anne from the late 15th century and one of the Virgin from the 16th century). At one end of the church there is a Romanesque chapel which was once used as a fortified refuge. Rising by the building is a fine square bell-tower.

General view of the Notre-Dame d'Espérance buildings overlooking the port of Cannes; details of the façade and of the bell-tower.

Entrance to the famous Fragonard factory in Grasse.

The Musée International de la Parfumerie.

Characteristic views of the town of Grasse.

GRASSE

The splendid town of Grasse is located only a few miles from Cagnes-sur-Mer and Antibes. Lying along the fascinating, steep ravines of the **Gorges du Loup,** it is a favorite destination for hikes and excursions among medieval villages and nearly uncontaminated oases of nature. But Grasse is also known as one of the world capitals of the perfume industry. All year round the air is pervaded by an endless succession of different fragrances: the essences of the mimosas, roses, lavender, jasmine flowers, violets and tuberoses blend with the scent of the orange blossoms to create an absolutely unique atmosphere. The cultivation of flowers, together with the companies whose work it is to transform products of foreign origin, are the area's major industrial resources.

A free city until 1227, Grasse allied with Pisa and Genoa; it later became a diocesan seat, and as such its influence grew until the time of the French Revolution. But the city owes its fortune above all to Caterina de'

The busy streets of Grasse.

Medici: the fashion of scented gloves launched by her in the 16th century sparked the transformation of Grasse from a tannery town known for its production of fine leathers to a center for the manufacture and trade of scents and aromatic essences. With the definitive divorce of the perfumeries from the tanneries, in the 18th century, Grasse established itself as a true leader in the former specialty.

Besides a tour of the industrial establishments, while in Grasse a visit to the **Musée International de la Parfumerie,** with its beautiful greenhouses of Mediterranean and sub-tropical plants, and to the **Fragonard Museum of Perfume,** is also a must. But the old city of Grasse also offers attractions more substantial than ethereal fragrance. Among other sights, the splendid 14th-century **Oratory Church** at the end of the charming **Rue de l'Oratoire**, lined with buildings in Italian Renaissance style, and the imposing 12th-century **Notre-Dame-du-Puy** cathedral. While being used as a storehouse for fodder in 1795, it suffered serious damage when it was nearly destroyed by a fire.

MOUGINS

This tiny town in the hills, with its enchanting view of the sea, is known above all for its excellent restaurants. Mougins, inhabited as early as Roman times and fortified in the 15th century, has since the 1930's been "rediscovered" thanks to such illustrious inhabitants as Pablo Picasso, Francis Picabia, Paul Eluard, Man Ray and Jean Cocteau.

Outside the town, a relaxing stroll takes us to the 16th-century **Chapel of Notre-Dame-de-Vie**, with its distinctive portico and beautiful expanse of green lawn.

A restaurant along the Mougins road.

LA NAPOULE

This delightful resort town boasts superb beaches of fine sand. The beautiful **fortress,** with its square towers, dates from the 14th century. It was restored by the American sculptor Henry Clews who left some of his works on display. The town is famous for its art exhibitions.

THÉOULE-SUR-MER

Protected by a promontory, this charming village has three fine beaches and a protected port for sail and motor boats. Along the seaside stands an odd crenelated building, flanked by turrets: an 18th-century soap factory which has now been turned into a castle.

La Napoule, the beautiful park enclosing the fortress.

View of the fortress of La Napoule, seen from the sea; panorama of the gulf of Théoule-sur-Mer.

The splendid cliffs of Anthéor.

Cap Roux with its distinctive crags rising from the sea.

ANTHÉOR

Who said the Côte d'Azur was just sandy or smooth-gravel beaches, framed by hills sloping gently down to the waters of the Mediterranean? Here and there, the coastline is broken by steeply rising cliffs on which the intense green of the vegetation suddenly gives way to red rocks - and the blue of the sea takes on rainbow reflections. Since the Anthéor seacoast offers one of the most suggestive panoramas in the entire area, it is a popular destination especially for the many small pleasure craft that set out from the nearby bathing beaches.

CAP ROUX

Like Anthéor, Cap Roux is one of the most attractive spots along the coast. The waters abound in underwater flora and fauna alike; the intensely-colored crags rising from the waters are home to numerous colonies of sea birds, which find here an ideal habitat and nesting site.
The main route to Cap Roux is by sea, and is an inviting alternative for those who want to escape from the crowded beaches of Cannes or Saint-Raphaël for a while.

LE TRAYAS

This pretty little resort has many stretches of beach, the largest of which is to be found in the **Figueirette** bay, which in the 17th century was a lively center for tuna fishing. You can also swim in the little baylets surrounded by red porphyry at the foot of hills all abloom with mimosa.

BOULOURIS

This quiet little town is actually a suburb of Saint-Raphaël. It is full of villas half-hidden among the pines, numerous beaches, and a little port. Nearby is **Dramont Beach**, on which the United States 36th Division landed on August 15, 1944.

AGAY

Agay is both a winter and summer resort, since it is well-protected between the **Pointes Longues** and the **Pointe de la Baumette**. It is renowned for its "roches rouges" (that is, the red porphyry of Estérel). On the lighthouse there has been set a plaque in memory of Antoine de Saint-Exupéry, the author of *Le Petit Prince*, who flew over Agay before disappearing into the sea the night of July 31, 1944.

Boats at anchor in the quiet waters of Agay.

The waters of Agay, where the pilot and celebrated writer Antoine de Saint-Exupéry crashed with his plane in 1944.

Le Trayas: a small port on the Figueirette bay.

SAINT-RAPHAËL

Saint-Raphaël has been a resort since ancient times, when the wealthy merchants of Fréjus came to spend their vacations here. The name San Rafeù appeared for the first time in the year 1043; the town was later fortified by the monks of St. Victor and again by the Knights Templar. During the French Revolution, the village took the name of Barraston, in honor of Barras. It was here that Napoleon triumphantly landed on his return from Egypt; but here also that he set sail for his exile on the Isle of Elba. The Allied landing of 1944 unfortunately greatly damaged the town.

Saint-Raphaël is situated on the Gulf of Fréjus, between **Pointe St. Aygulf** and the two red promontories called the **Lion de Terre** and the **Lion de Mer** (the land and sea lions). Its position is superb and its beaches splendid. The promenade, in the modern section of the town, is a major attraction and a favorite gathering spot. The double tourist port can handle up to 1800 boats

Eglise des Templiers (Church of the Templars)

This very interesting church, in the old city, was erected in the 12th century in the Provençal Romanesque style. The right apse was replaced by a square watch- and defensive tower, since the church was often used as a refuge during the frequent pirate attacks. The aisle- less interior boasts imposing supporting arches and contains a gilded wooden bust of St. Peter, which the fishermen carry in procession to the Lion de Mer on the August feast-day of their patron saint. On one side of the church is a paving slab of the ancient *Via Aurelia* and a fragment of the Roman aqueduct of Fréjus.

The Saint-Raphaël Beach

This fine sandy beach, even though not as luxurious as that of Cannes, is nonetheless quite attractive. Saint- Raphaël is the perfect place to spend a relaxing fami- ly vacation.

Saint-Raphaël. the Boulevard Général De Gaulle seen from the beach; while visiting the Côte d'Azur, one can try one's luck at the Saint-Raphaël Casino; a merry-go-round in the square in front of the Saint-Raphaël Casino.

The beautiful Church of the Templars, in Provençal Romanesque style.

Views of the magnificent Fréjus amphitheater.

Fréjus, the interior of the arena; bull-fighting in Fréjus.

FRÉJUS

Fréjus preserves the majority of the great architectural works raised there by the Romans. A diocesan seat since the year 374, and so strategically located that since the beginning of the Christian era its port had been second only to Marseilles in military and commercial importance, Fréjus' decline began in the 10th century, when the receding waters forced the town's economy to center primarily on land-based activities. The explosion of mass tourism determined the construction of the **Fréjus Plage** and **Port Fréjus** developments. Roman Fréjus is extremely important in terms of the number, variety and state of preservation of the remains.

The Amphitheater

The original amphitheater could hold from 10,000 to 12,000 spectators. The entranceways still exist, and in some cases are even mostly intact. The major axis measures 373.4 feet, while the minor one is 269.6 feet. The ground of the amphitheater has been so prepared as to be used for staging various types of shows and, during the summer months, even bullfights.

The ruins of the Roman theater of Fréjus.

The Aqueduct

This 31-mile-long aqueduct carried water from the Siagne River. Although it runs mostly underground, some surface stretches have arcading to cross over chasms.

The Roman Theater

The major axis of the theater measured some 236 feet; the minor axis 98.4. The stage and orchestra are still visible.

Porte des Gaules

This gate opened at the center of a half-moon flanked by towers on either side. Only the north tower is still standing.

The Porte des Gaules.

The aqueduct of Fréjus.

Fréjus, the ruins of the Porte d'Orée; Augustus' Lantern.

Augustus' Lantern

Another attractive sight is the stump of what is popularly known as the **Lantern** or **Tour d'Auguste**, an ancient lighthouse to which a chain was attached to close off access to the city from the sea.

La Porte d'Orée

La **Porte d'Orée,** of which some ruins remain, is one of the many sites in the western portion of the town that bear witness to the important role played by Fréjus during Roman times.

The Cathedral

The church is a fortified 10th century building with a plain but strikingly elegant bell-tower built two centuries later. The portal has fine Renaissance door posts.

Detail of the portal of the Fréjus cathedral; the cathedral square.

The inside of the church has a single nave of extreme simplicity and side aisle built in the 11th century in which there are a lovely wooden 16th-century Crucifix and two kneeling statues of the *Bishops of the Camelin Family* (uncle and nephew). Above the sacristy door is a lovely triptych by Jacques Durandi, a native of Nice, dated 1450.

The Baptistery

This is one of the oldest baptisteries still standing in France, dating back to the 4th or 5th century. Inside, the sides of the octagon are formed by alternating hollow and flat niches, set off by delicate black granite columns with capitals made of marble taken from the Roman forum of Fréjus.

Fréjus, the interior of the baptistery.

The nave of the Fréjus cathedral.

Port Grimaud: a miniature of Venice set in the Côte d'Azur.

The coches d'eau in one of Port Grimaud's most picturesque corners.

Pages 118-119: boats in the waters off Port Grimaud.

PORT-GRIMAUD

This town, like Nice, reminds one of Venice, with its ochre, yellow, and pink buildings, paved alleyways, tiny squares, canals, and the forms of the little foot-bridges that span them. Port-Grimaud is a modern lacustrine town created by the architect François Spoerry. Built at the end of the Gulf of Saint-Tropez, this little village of fishermen's houses, all brightly painted and no two alike, is undeniably of great appeal. By now, the houses which were put up in the 1960s are starting to show normal signs of age, so that they no longer have that just-built look. The heart of the village is a vast arcaded square which contains the local church, post office, and town hall. Restaurants and cafés enliven the scene. Just like in Venice, there are no cars in Port-Grimaud: you must park your car at the parking lot and continue either on foot or by boat, the equivalent of the Venetian *vaporetto* which here is known as the *coche d'eau* (water coach).

SAINTE-MAXIME

Straight across the bay from Saint-Tropez is Sainte-Maxime, a tiny town of about 8000 inhabitants, with a modern port offering well-equipped berths for small craft, a lively beach, a small **Casino** and beautiful gardens in which palms, mimosas and oleander trees create a shady oasis.

The huge anchor on the Casino Beach at Sainte-Maxime.

The modern bridge on the waterfront; in the background, the quiet beach of Sainte-Maxime.

Saint-Tropez, with its fascinating historic center, looks out over a splendid bay; the port hosts craft from world-over.

SAINT-TROPEZ

This is probably the most exclusive and snobbish resort along the Côte d'Azur. Nevertheless, during the off season the port and old city have a special appeal which is lacking in summertime when a strange cosmopolitan crowd composed of the famous and those aspiring to become so, real and fake artists, real and fake intellectuals, and the like, invade the town and set up headquarters in the port where the luxury yachts are anchored.

The economy, once based on fishing, is today almost totally reliant on tourism: the population of Saint-Tropez, in the winter months about 7,000, rises to almost 100,000 in the busiest season of the year.

The beach near Saint-Tropez.

*A painter shows his works on the docks; a quiet street
in the historic center of Saint-Tropez; typical establishments
on the Quai Suffren.*

*Historic automobiles along the docks of Saint-Tropez;
flowered balconies lining a street in the historic center.*

The Citadel that dominates the Bay of Saint-Tropez.

In the inner courtyard of the fort and along the bastions are interesting exhibits of historical weapons.

The Citadel

The first town center, of Roman origin, was totally destroyed in the 7th century when the Saracens sacked the region and murdered almost all its inhabitants. On the ashes of the old settlement there rose the **Citadel,** a fortified hamlet so strong it was able to withstand the attack launched against it by Spain's galleys in 1637.

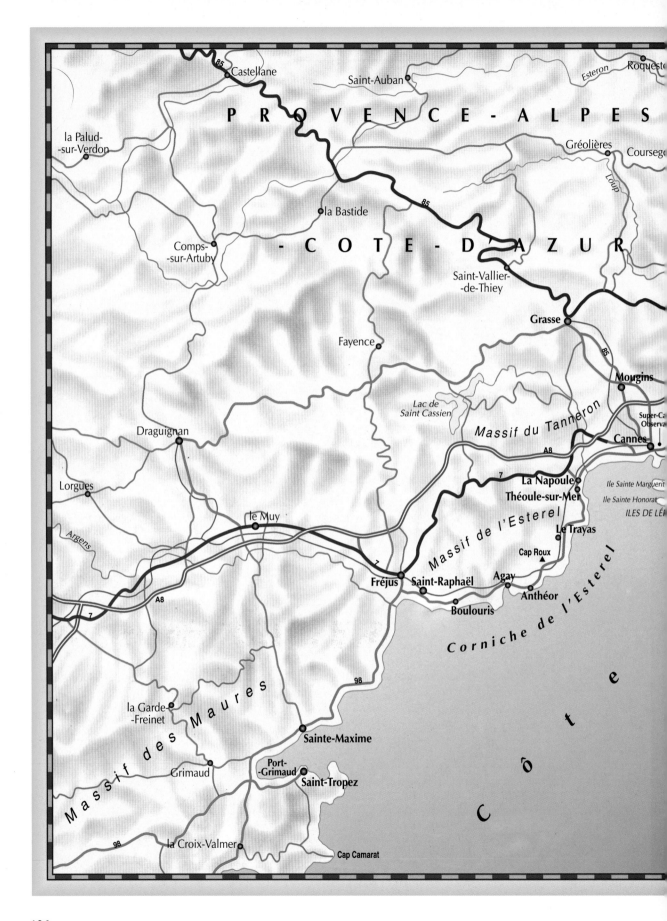

PROVENCE-ALPES

-COTE-D'AZUR

Castellane
Saint-Auban
Esteron
Roqueste
la Palud--sur-Verdon
Gréolières
Courseg
Loup
la Bastide
85
Comps--sur-Artuby
Saint-Vallier--de-Thiey
Fayence
Grasse
Mougins
Lac de Saint Cassien
Massif du Tanneron
Super-Ca Observa
Draguignan
A8
Cannes
7
La Napoule
Lorgues
Théoule-sur-Mer
Ile Sainte Marguerit
Ile Sainte Honorat
ILES DE LÉ
le Muy
Massif de l'Esterel
Le Trayas
Argens
Cap Roux
7
A8
Fréjus
Saint-Raphaël
Agay
Anthéor
Corniche de l'Esterel
7
Boulouris
Corniche de l'Esterel
98
la Garde--Freinet
Massif des Maures
C
ô
Sainte-Maxime
t
Port--Grimaud
Grimaud
Saint-Tropez
ô
98
t
C
la Croix-Valmer
Cap Camarat

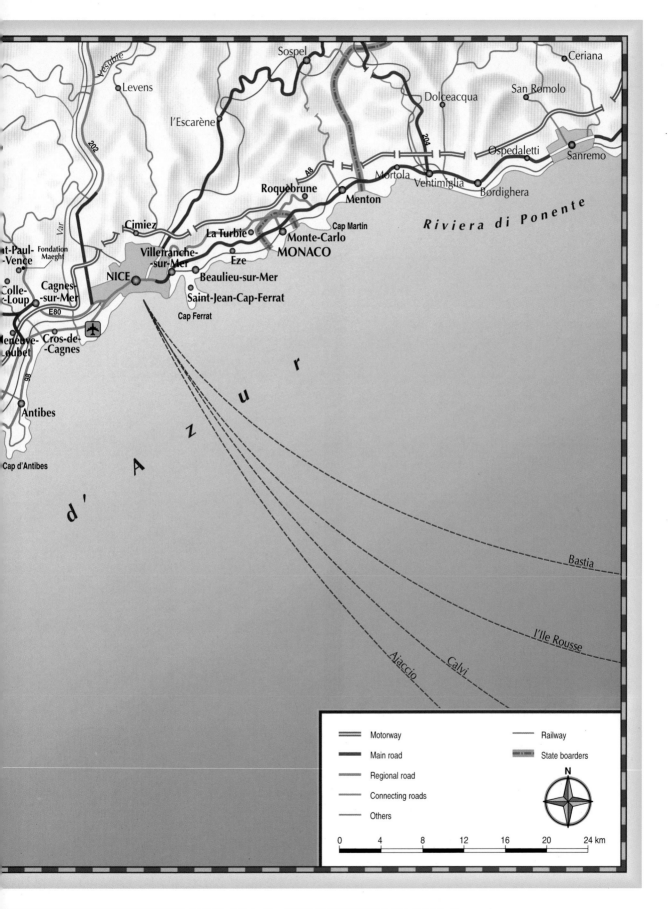

Levens

Vésubie

Sospel

Ceriana

San Romolo

Dolceacqua

l'Escarène

202

A8

204

Ospedaletti

Sanremo

Roquebrune

Mortola

Ventimiglia

Bordighera

Menton

Cap Martin

R i v i e r a   d i   P o n e n t e

Cimiez

La Turbie

Monte-Carlo

Villefranche-
-sur-Mer

Eze

MONACO

t-Paul-
-Vence

Fondation
Maeght

NICE

Beaulieu-sur-Mer

Colle-
-Loup

Cagnes-
-sur-Mer

Saint-Jean-Cap-Ferrat

Cap Ferrat

E80

eneuve-
oubet

Cros-de-
-Cagnes

98

r

u

z

Antibes

A

Cap d'Antibes

d'

Bastia

l'Ile Rousse

Ajaccio

Calvi

	Motorway		Railway
	Main road		State boarders
	Regional road		
	Connecting roads		
	Others		

N

0   4   8   12   16   20   24 km

INDEX